DEEP BREATHS

DEEP BREATHS

Leo Shelton

A Tugson Press Project

Deep Breaths – Poetry

All Rights Reserved © 2009 by United States Copyright Office—Library of Congress

No part of this book may be reproduced, transmitted, or utilized in any form or by any means, graphic, electronic or mechanical, including photocopying, recording, taping, or by any information storage or retrieval system, without the permission in writing from the publisher. Inquires should be addressed to Permissions, Tugson Press, Attn: Leo Shelton, P.O. Box 429, Temple Hills, MD 20757

Published by:
Tugson Press
P.O. Box 429
Temple Hills, MD 20757

Shelton, Leo.
Deep Breaths – Poetry / Leo Shelton.
ISBN: 0-9791786-4-9
1. Poetry, American. 2. Afro-Americans – Poetry. I. Title.

Printed in the United States of America
1ST Printing

Cover Design by Aaron Shelton

Don't just breathe ....breathe deeply!
—*The Author*

Contents

Breaths
I wonder You 11
Cry Country! 13
Infected 16
Kiss of Addiction 18
RANDOM 19
Today 21
My sonic 23
Untitled 25
Voice dance 26
Summer Love 27

Deep Breaths
Untitled 31
NOT TODAY 33
I BELIEVE IN LOVE 35
COULD YOU, WOULD YOU? 37
Two Towers 40
Hidden beaches 43
Like me? 46
INCREDIBLE 49
My kindred 51
Write me a love song 53

Whispers
Poet's Pen 57
What's a brutha to do? 59
Dream America 62
Who am I? 65
Undeserved Fame 67
Roots 69
Dad 71

Summer Rain 74
Brown Knight 75
CYCLIC 77

Murmurs
Miss Envy 81
Bridge 83
Mirror 85
Words 87
Faith 89
Birth of Soul 91
RAIN 93
Right 95
War 97
Crescent's center 99

Screams
AM 103
Player 105
Wrong 107
Cruise 109
Reliance 110
Her Blues 111
Jaded 114
Hate 115
Ewing 116
Speckling 118

Exhales
Breaths 123
Words 125
Indulge 127
And it's about 128
Wright 130
Aged 131
Surface 132
What death 133
Quest 134
Craven 135

About The Author 137

BREATHS

I wonder You

I wonder YOU
What you say
What you do
Today
To get through
'Til tomorrow is due

I wonder why
You bite your lips
And do that thing
With your eyes
And hide feelings so true

I wonder me
Thinking of YOU
Holding you tight
When you're out of my sight
But feel so close

And when I wish
And want
And touch
Myself

I wonder YOU
Wanting me,
Wanting You
Wanting Me
Then having YOU

I wonder when
My heart filled
So heavy with pride
And my soul moved your way
And why the music
You bring
Doesn't go away
And if it will?

I wonder YOU,
And I wonder how
These feelings so deep
And uncontrollable urges seep
Into all that I am
And sometimes I wonder
Outside myself
And into you,

Sometimes I do…

I wonder YOU

CRY COUNTRY!

Black as the night
Fallen in life
Hard
And bittered
Like the taste of pepper
And the smell
Of hatred
In hooded confines
Of hopeless cycles
Joined in misery
With others
Who have fallen in life?
And are black as the night
And bittered and hardened
And lack hope

Darkened minds
Where dreams
Of "blings"
Mask realities
Of empty stairs
And stairways
Leading to even darker

And more hopeless
Existence
Magnified by
Libations
And temptations
And depressive
Addictions
Started by
And resulting from
Minds darkened by dreams
Unrealized
And detoured paths
Leading to nowhere
Until the sun
Of a dark history
And a brighter future
Shadowed light
And knowledge
And truth
Magnified
Love
And faith
In people
In a world
Of darkness
Laying the bricks
Of a foundation
Of a new path
To new stairways
Leading to clarity
And out of despair

Crying country
Overcome!
Crying country
Overcome!

Infected

A meaningless action
Hidden in passion
Incomplete in deed
Mistakenly called love
Full of contradiction
And removed from proper context
More concerned with satisfaction
And interaction
And who's better?
What's next?

Long on a rope
Short on depth
Moments in time
Hanging on words
Lifetimes behind
Moments of foolish lust
Cashed in
On a bitter wind
Of chance and pleasure
That changes the face
And place
Of YOU in this world

Forever!

Infect knowledge
Share truth
Love others
As self
And spread this word!

Kiss of Addiction

Fanatically addicted
To muscles, masculinity and all that madness
Lifestyle dreams
Don't mean a thing to me
Just give me the sensations of love
With sweat dripping
And kisses, til my lips are parched
And chapstick runs the other way
Where I'm passing the day
In some arms and loins and hugs and kisses
Daytime wishes
Of those nighttime kisses
The ones that smooth
And break rules
Where skillz are like tools
And defy belief
And underneath
Sweat meat
Are big feet
And warm, warm kisses
Naked embraces
Sucking faces
And other places
Fanatically addicted
To the kisses

RANDOM

But Life is not random
    Nor defined
It doesn't flow
    Like the big blue open sea
But its beauty is just as clear
And sometimes it roars like the wild
    And soars like eagles
    Blissful, yet sometimes vile
But never unworthy of another's
    Look or stare
    Adventure or dare
    Or dream or wish or challenged goal
    Or the chance to turn new things old
And to touch
    To feel
    To love and hold
Then kiss again
Or tap earth and wind
Or fire within
For the mere existence of life
Before winter, spring and summer ends
And begins, and begins, and begins
Yet again

Is life in its sweetness defined?
And experienced, and cherished
And breathed, and lived
Forever….randomly.

Today

Today, I found my way
    Back in the times
    Back in the day
Where I could almost touch
A past that waited on
The calendar to turn
It burned
A place in my heart
    Of a day
    Like yesterday
When I smelt your hair
Like you were there
And felt a love
Like Grammy's hug
And saw your smile
And for a little while
    Saw the sun's rays
    And clouds dancing
Like back in time
When you were mine
Before that day
You went away
    And my tomorrow's stopped

And became…
Yesterdays….
Just like today
Tomorrow?

My sonic

Is 40 years minus 1 lifetime?
Hanging on with both hearts
With a hand full of happiness
And one almost full of despair
To songs once sung
And melodies that wait for artists to articulate their heartbeats
Background noise
To life's dance
And blue notes
And diamond droplets
Mimicking stars
And tears of joy
Hidden in choices
And mistakes
Made again
When the pitch or the beat
Calls for new buds and flocks
To blossom again
Until new suns rise
And new surprises ride
Into the heart and the day
Of new dreams

No thoughtless thing
In my summer springs
Or autumn's clock
Tick

Untitled

No drink of wine
Or kiss in time
Was ever quite as sweet

And no waking morn
Have I ever slept?
Without 'least your heart-touch
By my side

Not in dreams lived
Or hope cherished
Or even relished pasts

Not ever has "forever"
Had a face
And a name
And a touch
So much

Voice Dance

Breathing in your heartbeats
Like smooth jazz
Sprinkled with trance rhythms
Merged with tribal beats
Overlaid with rap
Shafted with reggae

Transfixed on your tongue dance
With your lips and your mouth
As my ears kept beat
And my body fell limp
And my clothes unbound
Themselves

My spirit connected
And my heart fluttered and danced
To the rhythms and beat of your murmurs
Lifting my libido
And my curiosity
For what it was that you actually said

What was it that you actually said?

Summer Love

My Summer Love
Blazing through,
Well, like the sun
Into the darkest corners of morning
Rising and reeking havoc
At 6:69…
That's 7 AM plus that 10 minute snooze
Almost
Raising the dead from miserable sleeps
And steep, and deep dreamlands
That duck
And hide from, well…life
Dancing through like stars
Twinkling twice as bright
Orbiting earthlings
Targeting me
Racing, then slowing
Scorching and hot but calming
Joy bringing…
And got me singing
About seasons that never change
And that's why Summer Loves last forever
For reasons

Unknown
Then they leave
Or come back
And repeat

Deep Breaths

Untitled

Ain't never much cared
For long roads,
They remind me of places
I'll never go and things
I'll never see

Ain't never cared much for short songs
That teases the heart
But leave you even more
Lonely

Ain't never much cared
For expensive things
Or day dreams
I'd rather save them for nights

Never wanted to be shorter
Or even taller
But thinner, well
I might

But not fabulous
Or grand
Not a martyr

Just a man
Centered by heart
And smart
Where flowers grow 'round
And not even storms or floods
Or journeys
Abound
Stand in the way of destiny
For me

NOT TODAY

I want to believe…
That there's no place special
That I haven't been
And that there's no time worth having
No breath worth breathing
That doesn't contain your DNA

I want to hope…
Those days without me
And days without you
Don't turn pages of the calendar
Don't become moments
Or seconds,
Or minutes
Or complete days….

I want to wish
For a complete replay of time
When birds and chirps
Echo in time
And ecstasy highs

Remain sublime
Even after you've walked away

I want to know
That waking up
Looking up
Reaching up
And falling asleep
Is all a part of the day?
And the way
That we love

But what I believed
And hoped,
And wished,
And the essence of what I knew,
Has passed like the season
With convoluted reasons
Into what is
And IS not
Your way…
Not for me
Not for another
Not TODAY!

I BELIEVE IN LOVE

The kind that sustains you when nothing else matters
Nothing else warms you or embraces your being
When nothing but LOVE and the feel of LOVE makes life
Tolerable
Livable
Even LOVEABLE

AND, I believe in grace
The kind that works with karma
The kind that makes you give everything you got
And accept what comes your way, because you did the right thing…
I believe in floating in
And bowing out
GRACEFULLY
Knowing that you have done the right thing
And been the right type of person
To yourself as well as others

I believe in respect
And balance of mind, body, spirit
Coupled with a thirsty desire
For exploration and learning
And the individual meaning of life

Through love and understanding
Acceptance and non-judgment
Through everyday steps toward blending into this world
And being a part of it,
But only in a way that exercises the right and necessity
To be different from it

Yep, I believe in LOVE
And life, and its pursuit
Never ending, never settling
Growth and mistakes
Exploration for the sake
Of finding yet another road
Another path
And another lesson of life

I believe in YOU!

COULD YOU, WOULD YOU?

IF someone told you life was the dress rehearsal
For the ultimate reward which was death...
Would you believe them?
Would you do anything different?

IF they told you that it is not the toys you collect
Or the designer clothes you buy
Or the clothes and degrees you had at the end
But what you entered the white gates of plantation
Not called the Bahamas, but ever so beautiful

Would you work on the non-material things that you could take with you?
Or the naked body that you would display as you waited hopefully for a white cloak and wing fitting?

Would you tattoo the good things you have done,
In the life you've lived, here on this earth
Or plant the seeds of love in others
And let that stand as the testament of your contributions of a world not without you, but just rid of your nakedness?

WOULD you go back and marry yourself?
Date your self?
Have kids of your own?
Like you?
With you?
For you?

Would you waste precious time criticizing the shortcomings of those who didn't meet your expectations?
Or spend that time in gratitude for the experiences had?

Would you hit pause on the good and rewind on the bad, to make sure you learned the lessons?
Or live it all in fast-forward, with no regrets and no apologies?

Could LOVE be an action world in your vocabulary?
An addiction of deeds,

A force of purpose?
Or would it still be and endless pursuit
Of dream-like movies?

Would you, could you,
Love yourself enough
That others compliment your life
And not become it?

Could you be comfortable loving you?

Even when no one else is?

Could you cry, and dream
Know what it means
Explore and yearn
Breathe and learn
All in anticipation
And preparation
For one day sharing it with another?
Even if that person never arrives?

Could you stand on the stage of life,
Naked as you are
And be comfortable
Really comfortable
With what is not?

Could you live today?
To die tomorrow?
Without the hope of anything more?

Could you write these words
In your own truths
As a declaration to your life?
Would you?
Could you?

Two Towers

Two
Towers
of
strength

Two
Towers
of
pride

Reflecting
A love of life
A coming together
But separation of classes
Of people
Of countries
But a commitment to principles

Freedom
Of expression
And celebrations of choices
Through Windows of the world
And pictures of hate

Actions of a few
Reflected in the lives
And loss of lives
Of many
Clandestine sounds
And horrors spoke in grimaces
Hate spoken in actions
And yet no words
Just deeds

Real life horror
And reflection
Introspective reflection
Of a bad dream
A wake-up call
A redefining day
Of honor
And respect
For freedoms
Taken for granted
In a poetic sketch
Of good and evil

Towers
Of
strength

Towers
of
pride

Demolished by hate
Restored by love
And
new
towers
of
strength

And
Towers
Of
pride

Erected in history
Forever

Hidden beaches

Built of sugar cane
Sony sounds
Inspired
By the sweet taste of honey
That sticks like molasses
As smooth as Jazz
And the gift of Vaughn
Hipped up
With a lot of hop
Then thrown down
Like the waves of water
Landing on hidden beaches

"Beyond words"
"Beyond SOUNDS"
And sometimes, just BEYOND belief
"Exclusively" mine
And yours
Oh, "it's love"
Getting in the way of life

Vibe kisses
And big ole
Surrounding hugs

You know
The ones
Like that hidden beach

The hold
And control
Of sweet epiphanies
Trapped in the middle of my now
Raining down like love
Transfixed on my being
Watching me
Showing me
Hidden beaches

Inner flows
Manipulated rapture
Like jazzy sensations
Of impeding rides
To places low
And high

Key strokes
Smoke screens
Of past loves
And losses
Rapped in moments of pain
And of crystal love
Unwrapped in sounds

Paintings
And poetry
Amused
By the muse
Of past meets present
And present moves onward
All in step
All on key

Like the music of life
And rhythms of love
Should be
And seem
To be
In tune
With heart beats

Like me?

The roots of my hair
Will take care
To explain the flare
In my nose
And the slope of my rear
Maybe

But the glare
From my stare
Off my hues
Or size of my shoes
Reveal less
Than more
About me

And my height
And towering sight
Just might
Reveal more about my strength
Internally
Than externally
You see?

Is it no surprise?

Deep Breaths

That my eyes
Reflect the shape of the heart
In the mirrored image
Of my country
Unbelievably
Indescribably
Unique

Seems weird
To me at least
To believe
That I've never
Ever
Really
Been home-
Are you?
Like me?
Write it on the wall
And call it a song
And play that note
That I could read blindly
Sing it out like an ocean
Tides racing over lips
Penetrating loins
Like Earth and Wind
Fire up the hook

Release all pain
And rain down on me
Sweet song of love

Echo in my psychic
Move me to tears
And before I've had a chance
To actually cry
Surround me
Embrace me
Touch me
Like a circle of one

Pick me up
And spin me around
In the rapture of life
And song
And love
And music

And just when I've melted
In the beat and the groove
Change beats
Change the rhythm
Change my heart
And make me dance again

Make me dance again!

INCREDIBLE

But UNDERSTANDABLE
How we don't work LOVE
But LOVE works wonders
And we work the plan
Of another MAN
Or WOMAN

INVISIBLE
But CONCEIVABLE
How KHARMA delivers
The FATE of the UNKOWN
But the truth of character
To those who believe
In such things

WONDERFUL
But SCARY
When loving yourself
Takes precedence
Over loving others

And leaves us
WANTING
NEEDING
DESIRING
EVEN more

CRAZY
But TRUE
How LONLINESS
Often means being without
But SELFLISHNESS
Means being amongst OTHERS
And connecting needs
And wants
And desires
And LOVE connects the dots
And dots the "EYE's"
Of both

INCREDIBLE
But UNDERSTANDABLE
INVISIBLE
But CONCEIVABLE
WONDERFUL
But SCARY
CRAZY
But TRUE
LOVE

My kindred

My kindred spirit
Old and mature
Beyond its years
As if
Spirits age

Insatiable
Ever changing
Growing
Spiraling
Searching
Absorbing
Life

Heart felt
Heart beats
Unconnected
Connections
Linking Love
To Lust
And Lust to Life
And life to the loss
Of yesterday

And new connections
To Today
And tomorrow

Soaring
Sizzling
Life chains
Of connected spirits
That substantiates purpose
Solidifies meaning
Justifies existence
And confirms faith

My kindred spirit
My shared heart
Not even my own

Write me a love song

Write me a love song
In the pitch of life
Hot like candles
And dripping wax

Write me a love song
Of your own accord
Where they flow like cream
Every word

Just write me a love song
Nothing special
Nothing spectacular
As simple as like
But lust like strong

Sing it loud
And make the words clear
Use all those pet words
Every one but "Dear"

And write it as a duet
Crazy bridges and hooks

Hot like fire
But the sympathy of crooks
Write me that love song

No commercial hype
No music of any particular type
No special flow
And no ones has to know
That it's a long song
Just for me!

WHISPERS

Poet's Pen

Spoken words
They spoke easy
With words of contentment
About a love never endured

The spoke softly
With the exercised control of a musical lyricist
But with the immediacy of lust in their yes
And their hearts

The spoke calmly
About a world that consider them less
And meaningless
Yet, they still spoke
And spoke gracefully

They spoke proudly
Of their differences
And gayness
Or despair
And measurable and purposefully differences
Of the status-quo
And wore cloaks of armor

To ignorance
And violence
And hate
And fear

They spoke loudly
Very loudly
About acceptance
And joy
And love and human
But not special rights

They spoke poetically
About a nature and race
And people united
In acceptance and respect
In love and not fear
In understanding and not hate
In affirmation and not sympathy
In unity of hearts, and deeds, and actions
And words

They spoke and wrote
So that their words would be recorded
Forever
And spoke and spoke
Over and over again

They spoke the words
From a poet's pen

What's a Brutha to Do?

When greatness is demanded
What's a brutha to do?
When perfection is required...
Like a suit and tie luncheon,
Or access is denied
What's a brutha to do?
When he must deliver, decide
Or stand by the side
And wish he were someone
Worthy of a reservation
In the line of YOUR choosing
NOT others
What's a brutha to do?
When the world has picked up the crayons
And repainted your golden brown hue
With blackover colors
And connected stereotypical dots
To dots and lines
That DO NOT apply
On a palate that is already full
Of a shadowed pride
With hourderves of self-doubt

What's a brutha to do?
When he carries the weight of a race
And the human race
On the shoulder of ancestors
Forging Forward
BECAUSE of "the path that has been paved for him"
Doing all the "right" things
Only to discover
That the road is clouded by trees
And roadblocks have been strategically placed
In the middle of roads
With his name and the name of his brothers
Along the parkways of life
With detours like drugs
Or jail…Or fame…
But not with words like "CEO" or "president"
Or even "the game"
Not even "the piece of the pie"
Or "the heaping serving of life"
Not "behind this door"
Or even "destined for greatness"
So, what's a brutha to do?

What IS a brutha to do?

Become the cliché that has created at least a part of him?
Maybe the part that he cannot change?
Become a little more bitter and aggressive
Wear his "street" and "hood" in his walk?
In his talk?
In his art and his craft?

Redeem himself with his race
By becoming a new "breed" of haves?
Who have not?

A role model
To anyone who happens to still be looking for one?

Redefine SUCCESS
Not by degrees that he holds
But by the bank roll he folds
Doing it HIS way?

So, when he blazes through
Stealing from you and me
And a generation yet to be
Or if he's just stilling moments and ideas
And strategizing internally
And it doesn't seem like he's moving progressively
Maybe he just doing what he has to do
To hold fast, be strong and work it thru
So, UNDERSTAND…
NO DISRESPECT…
NO MOTIVE TRUE…

He's just doing….
What a brutha has to do!

Dream America

Dream America
Of something bigger than yourselves
Something different than you and your friends
Your neighbors and congregations

Dream of a world
Where everyone is rich
Or better yet, everyone is poor

Dream of your kids and your loves and your life
In a different color and hue
Dream of a "them" replaced by "you"

Dream of board rooms that truly represent the clients
And courts of law where the letter of the law
Offers the same flexibility and creativity as the spirit of the law

And dream of religions blended
And honored and celebrated
And no race boxes to check
Or genders or ages

Where John and James
And Lena and Lorrie
Say "I do"
And no one tells them that
"They won't"
And they enjoy the life and liberty
And their own personal pursuit of happiness

Where the health of a nation
And the budget for it
Is always greater than our assistance
Or loans
Or political donations to any other country
Where we stand together against
The real terrorist
Outside of our door and on our block
In corporate disguises
And even civil servants

Where the First Amendment
Holds the same credence
As the espoused selection of verse
That becomes the counter arguments
Of discussions with people
Who don't even have the same beliefs?

Dream America!
Not of how far we have come
But for how far we could go
If we only believed
And loved

And continued to dream
And live the dream
America!

Who am I?

Who am I,
If not the person you see
The person I show
The one you don't know
Who am I?

Who am I,
If not the person in the mirror
Staring back
With questions
About confidence
And tact
But sizing you up
With me
To me

Who am I,
If not a small piece of you
And you
And you
Looking back at me
And wondering you

And who are you?
If not but to ask
Or even care
Or inquire
Why I am?
Who am I?
Then, Who are you?

Undeserved Fame

Credit me with that image of buster
A hustler, a homie from the hood
And write me a character profile
With a docile
Of warrants and bad doings
Craft my death and life plan
And include a helping hand
From birth to the hood of man
Like you landscaped my dwellings
And my lack of respect
For my home
Simply called "The projects"

Slow up my evolution
And raise me to the top
Kill my revolution
Whenever it begins or stops
To wait for reality to catch up with what really is....
Foster the imagery and myth
That I am bigger than life
Oh, yeah, much bigger than life
Hiding the strife
Of what it is like

To have so much
And yet so little

Garner my personal strengths
By paying me for my physical ones
And when I'm done
Pay me again
So that I continue to be entertainment
For the masses
And so that it still passes
As separate
But equal

Damn, I can only imagine what a black man in America is like…
Sike….
But thank God, I'm an actor.

Roots

My roots are a safe place
External as well as internal
They run as long as the Cumberland River
And as deep as the values of Look Out
Within a family, a community, a culture

They take shape in the twang in my voice
In the jive in my walk
Or the greetings of elders
Or defense of my origins
Strangely, but uniquely from my own individual but collective perspective

Spreading out like limbs of a tree
Full of diversity
And connected spirits
But strangely, uniquely
Connected and separated all at once

It is who I am,
Who I'm supposed to be
How others see me
What I would like others to see

And the reality of what is…
And what is not!

These are my roots!
Tying me to what was,
Giving me the range to come into what is
Connecting me to what will be,
And grounding me in all possibilities, challenges,
Humbling me in life and self

Dad

My Warrior
Like a Saint
Like Vincent de Paul
Come on y'all
A Jubilee
From Tennessee
Dark berries
Sweet trees
And bee-bees

A Knight
Like Peter Clever
A negotiator
A definite
Smile maker
Ya'll know what I'm talking about

A thick pillar of strength
Condensed
To a beating valve
But only one half
Of a wonderful union

A momma's boy
But undeniably joy
Of his Big Daddy's heart
And smart
And always a part
Of all the right things
From the start

A Tiger
Without the purr
But for sure
A man
Pure
Who stood higher than mountains
And wider than seas
For those he loved
And those in need

A father
A friend
A confidant
A credit to family
And race
And humanity
And then…
Some

An example setter
A Life better
In all the best things in people
And their word

A Sword
Protector
Peacemaker
For a small piece of this mad world

An incredible man
For anyone to call Dad
…especially for me!

Summer Rain

Ain't nothing like Summer Rain
Washing away pains
Caused by longer than life
Winter LOVES
Nothing like that summer rain

Humility's tears
Endured
Like seared sidewalks
Interrupted small talks
But refreshing spirits
With new growth
And life with new liberties
Nothing like those summer rains

Nothing like those summer rains
Flowing down faces
Like the smiles of a kids joy
Something to see
But even something more
Like an adults lust
It's like a must
During those summer rains
Oh, those summer rains

Brown Knight

Black Night
Every thing about you is dark
Like the shadow of moons
After long summer days
Like long pauses of silence
After the wrong things to say
Dark like the berries
Sweet like the juice
The horrible reality of lies
The strange comfort of truth

A complex and ironic rainbow
In a storm of life, and thunder
Forever unpredictable
Keeping us wondering
If there really is something whack
About black
And whether it is empty
And without color
Or a combination of hues
That defines me
And YOU

Brown nights
Black Knights
Something peaceful about the darkness
Something scary about your unknown
Something magnificent about power
Your strength
And the fabric you've woven
In the song you've sung
And the tapestry you've sewn
In your life, your hood,
Your world
And OURS!

CYCLIC

LOVE!
Misunderstood?
Oh, must be nice
Because you could
Or would NOT?
Take the time
To find the line
To tow
To pull
To walk
And to manage it
To talk through it
To grow in it
And know within it
That it's defined
And sublimed
In the minds
Of those who contribute it
LIVE in it
LOVE in it
And measure it not by what you get out
But by what you give in

MISUNDERSTOOD?
It should
Could?
Would!
Be whole
And grown
And fully developed
By now
If only you had taken the time
To find the line
To tow
And pull
And walk
And manage
And talk
And defined it
In your mind
And mine?

In a way that you UNDERSTOOD
And LIVED in it!
And LOVED in it!
For a little while longer…

Murmurs

Miss Envy

Miss Envy, long gone and forsaken
Ill willed and jealous
Possessed by desires
And self failings
Projected covets
Rejected truths
She ain't what she wants to be or ought to be
She is what she is
NOT

Miss Envy, begrudging reality
Living outside of herself
Housed in the temporary space of death
Challenged by contempt
Inspired by mirrors
Seen through crooked eyes
And a deep despise
For those who not only dare to live
But to dream

Ole Miss Envy
Gone for now
Forsaken always

Departs
But returns
With a vengeance
In search for yet another target
And another temporary space
To possess
And rest
On her loans

Bridge

Bridge of my fate
My faith
My state of being
Connecting
Transcending
Time
Again
Rippled life waves
And flows
And currents
And events
Reflective on marble stone
But not alone
Shadowed columns
Of dignity and pride
Hide
Beneath the truffles

And in the distance
Underneath
Beyond the feet
Life expanded
Embodied

And reached
Then repeated
New Heights
New Challenges
New beats

And connected
And transcended
My fate
My faith
My life
One more time
Unabridged

To new bridges
And across new seas
Again, and Again, and Again.

Mirror

In a world filled of calamity
Distorted images of gayety
And peaceful initiatives question choice
Or environment or nurture
Poke holes in Mother Nature's creativity
And cover mirrors
And eyes
And minds
Like Shiva

In a world so open and free
Where we fight for freedom
And diversity
But look at ourselves
And can't see others
As we see
Ourselves
So differently

A world so spectacular
So different,
So incredible in design
And yet we can't find

So much of Thee
In you
In me
In We
Together!

Words

WORDS so nice,
I said 'em twice ya'll
So nice,
I said 'em twice
I SAID THEM TWICE!
HUGS so tight
I lost my might
To hold my self upright
Tight!
Messing with my might
A real DELIGHT!
KISS so WET
I was drowning ya'lll
Wiped out,
Like a surfer looking for higher
Ground
Or Waves
And the RUSH ya'll
The TOUCH ya'll
And I thought nicotine
And oral fetishes
Were addictive!
That presence ya'll
That says I'm here…

And you're here TOO
Right now!
AND IT'S OK!
And this moment
This REFLECTION in mirrors of now
And windows of more
And this CONNECTION,
PROTECTION,
This self-isolating
GOOD thing!
That's pulling us in…
Pulling us close,
Separating NOW
From two minutes ago
And 8 minutes from now
And 10 years from now

Becomes IRRELEVANT to this moment
This INTER-COURSE
And everything else….
BUT
This JOY
This PAIN
This FEAR
And this LOVE
That WE have made
TOGETHER!

Faith

Twelve and grown
But not
Growing up too fast and hot
Begotten by sprits and innocence
Gone
Never lost
Never disowned
…just Stollen!
By those who study the word of GOD
No less
But follow the spirit of His law
At best
In daylight hours
Behind textured windows
And French doors
And flowers and candlelight music
And stages and pews
But more brothel
Than sanctuary
More scary than morning after
More death behind eyes
Than bravery behind souls
More long-reaching than religion

And more lethal than war
More permanent than love
More or less, and less and yet more
And more and more and more
Less like death living
Kneeling…and crawling…
Stumbling and crawling
And mumbling all the while…
Yes Daddy, boys get raped too
"Yes, Daddy, boys do get raped too!"

Birth of Soul

Lovable
So very lovable
Plugged-in
To my resistant cynic
But there
And so lovable
Like gospel music
And second breaths
Deeper
And more powerful than the desire to dance
Even inappropriately
In streets naked
And shadowed in insecurity
More me than my taste
More you than a smile
More definite than time
Spatially defined
And amazing yet more complicated
Than words can articulate
Or should…
Lovable,
Personable,
Collectively grateful

And giving
And reborn
Again
And again
And again
Through connections deep
And well,
Lovable
Souls

RAIN

It flowed like tears
Pouring
Smothering biscuit fed cheeks
Then dissolving
Like old loves
Robbing
Hearts of necessary energy
Never calming
Not making stronger
Just sorrow sweating
Perspiring
Desiring
Time to come back
And heal wounds
Feel balloons
Before parties began
Before clouds covered
Lightening discovered
Parties to crash
Like rivers of Nile
Denied
Chance
And possibilities

Of anything but perfect days
Perfect days
Without it

Right

Poetically mused
Even amused
And yet challenged
Sometimes
To write lines
Not that defines
Or shapes
But adds meanings
To things
Already connected
Dis-connected
Yet already in harmonic perspective
Blissful and fine
Like a moonlights shine
And a shadow of rainy suns
Pieces of hearts
Locked in art
And portraits spanning time
Distributed in time
And lives

And loves
And sorrows
Sometimes too deep to describe
Too easy to subscribe
Too wonder and full not to try
To put into words
Rhythms danced
Music heard…
Live breathed in
Then out…

War

My Rwanda
Your Iraq
Latino's on homefronts
Under Attack
And they preach and they teach
About taking values back

My DC
And your PG county
Your Bethesda
And Fairfax county

My rights
My fight
Your humane
Never the same
Trading fate
For your hate

And my rap
And my jazz
And your rock
And our roll

And our souls
Our country
Our home

…not so free?

Crescent's Center

Amongst chaos and simple pleasures
Deep below the crescent's center
In the darker hues of black and blue
And crimson flows that radiate through
Stands little boys and little girls
In big ole' worlds full of toys
And play-days and sunlit days
Flicker through calendar mazes
And violet hazes
And life stuff too deep to inhale
That pales in comparison to what was or could be
Mirroring times like fine wines
Maturing as we do
But too busy ducking death
Quacking too loudly and strokes too short
And momentum too fast
To enjoy life's ride
Too full and too hungry
To sit at the table
And eat
And enjoy
Together or alone

Screams

AM

Deep in my intellect
But above my introspect
I know
And it shows
That I am
Somebody

Some shade of hue
Darker than me
But compared to others
Now I see
That I am
Somebody

Somebody more than my self
Something more than books on a shelf
A righted wrong
Smart
And strong
I am

Prized in the eyes
Of my father's father

Because somebody bothered
To be
Just like
Me

Paved ways
Of my sojourn
And yours
Too
Yeah
You
Too

Debt owed
Of a price paid
Laid down
In white gowns
Of Blood
Now freedom floods
Through bodies of some
More

Player

Sample me silly
As I flirt through
Suggest and entice too

Laugh me painfully
Tickle me blue
Kiss and hold and release me
Make it true

Whisper in ecstasy
Travel me far
Torture and hurt me good
Leave not a scar

Educate me through poetry
Dance within silence
Intoxicate
And motivate
Through praise

Talk to me slowly
Reveal who you were
And who you are and will or try to be

With
And without me
Asking

Accept complements
Never supplement
Or substitute
Absolutely
Be you
And let me
Be you
Too

Wrong

Cum Laude
Laude dade Laude
Hit the lottery with this one
A smarty
Hearty
Corn-fed strong
Long and wrong
Even when right
Out of sight
Sick to death
Full of that wealth
Undefined in this world
By swords of words
Like worlds of curds
Without the absurd
Whiling out
Crossing borders
I hear ya
And I feel ya
When the light bulb went out
When that light bulb went out
Didn't have to shout
To make the point

And can hide politics in this joint
For the ones who look for meaning
Between the stitching and seaming
Of worlds that only seem
Redeemed
Of words that only seem
Without a means

Cruise

Having had some summer night days
I rejoice at comets dim and raised
Wake to rays of in jubilant praise
As though I had never slept or lazed

Songs of joy inside my head
Fighting back dances instead
Stretching out like branches dead
This is not even my bed
This is not even my bed

Hailing cabs with moonlit seats
Replete with icy sheets
Joyous but not complete
I have become one with streets
This is fantasy discrete

Regrets that never enter my mind
Care I carefully leave behind
This day has ended more than fine
I left behind
I left behind
Mine

Reliance

In stark contrast
Existence doesn't last
But excelling does
In simple things achieved

In complete defiance
Lack of reliance
Defaults to lack of feedback
And therefore
Reciprocation

In total clarity
Nothing but charity
Really gives back
Unless it is love
Unless
It is unconditional

Her Blues

Downhearted blues
From deep down in Chattanooga
Celebrate Miss Bessie Smith
While they torture and torment,
With the facts that "yo man don't love you"
At least not as much as yo blues
And love keeps dragging you down
Distinctively and soulfully
Concentrated in sessions
Of the likes of Billie, on holidays
And regular days
Subtle and mellow
Yellow and mellow
Undeniably blue
In a spiritual swing
They mean things
Deep inside ya
Like Ida
Coxing and boxing
With love things
Ballads as sweet as
Sisters named Bessie Smith
And Dinah Washington

Fused articulation
Matriculation
Without hesitation
Branding ones who dare
To love so deeply
Love bound in notes
Carried like totes
From heart to heart
Jazzy blue beats
Covering comfortable life seats
Cause you in love
Cause you in love
And Ethel Waters
And Lena Horn
And other sophisticated ladies
Save the day
In singing the prayers
That we all pray
When we're in love
When we're in love
Life imitating life
Music delivering dreams
Through stormy weathers
And peaceful streams
To cabins in the sky
"Have a good time, no longer down"
And then there's Ruth Brown
With country blues
Earthy and sympathetic
As life can be
When people like Helen Hughes

Join the court, and takes on the plea
But nothing like the cries
The tears that rise
In every eye and soul
When AIDS sings
When AIDS sings
Her song
Her message true
Just like her blues
Just like her blues

JADED

And they made obsession
Less than sweet
A coveted symptom
A fault and retreat
From real love
Real life
Real emotions
Spent
Investments
In monogamy and commitment
And now that time has passed
And love did not exist
Or last
The chance of time
The intent of mine
I am spent
I have no sense
No cents to reinvest
In past tense
No sense to reinvest
In what love represents

HATE

Self love beseeches thee
Parlays in agony
Begged to be seen
And loved and fed
And instead of butterfly
Land
Like a back hand
It can grow like yeast
And that love is a beast!
If not carefully released
Or absorbed;
It swirls and twirls
Like a hidden pearl
In the middle of you
And middle of oceans
Blue
Not murky but clear
And steers you away
Hunts you down
Calls your name
And all the same
Bows,
Tilts his hat
And disappears…

Ewing

Ewing
Summer solstice
White sand oceans
Life in perfect motion
Winter shinning
Sun piercing
Wind so strong
And fall decorative
Couture
Deep as the color
Outline and echo
Stitched and sewn
Loud as the drum
Insignificance
Fabric
A vessel
Defined by greatness
Hauteur
In perfect pitch
Outlined in goodness
And belted
Orchestrated by the maestro
Filled with music
Singing

Harped
Ewing
Proud
Perfection

Speckling

My run ins with run ins
Has made my dance weak
Yet my bravado
My solo still strong
I belong here
In this place
I have breathed it in
Sucked it out
Savored the flavors
Washed them out
I have
Carved this place out
Named it
Even when shaming it
Called it mine
This mind, this body
This soul
Mold out more than some
Less than many
And a small speckling of what
Collectively
We are all that is good
And bad and sad

And happily
Sometimes disgustingly
You and me
Not so perfectly
Not so strangely
Unique
But we are beautifully
US

EXHALES

Breaths

Shadows of sunny days
Lazy incentives to pray
To say thank you
And magnificent
And well done
And it's okay
Even if it rains today

Rainbows of yesterday
Casting spells
On word play
Like brilliant
Wonderful
In fabulous ways
And it's okay
If it dissolves away

Rainy tomorrows
Filled with sorrows
Until
Rainbows of sunny days
And shadows of yesterday
Blend in some incredible way

And make it okay
To breathe again,
Deeply!

Words

And he must detest
Find it hard not to reject and disregard
Those who have no respect for words
Cause I'm sure you've heard
They mean things
Define beings
Transcend meanings
And make everything gorgeous
And beautiful, and lovely and even those things
Mean different things
In the words we've heard
From those who communicate verse
Peruse a dichotomy of truths
That must play like symphonies
To those who listen
That really listen!

And he must curse
Those whose diverse yet shallow repartee
Makes conversations yawn
And relationships not work
If only through give and take
For heaven's sake

Words!
Simple words!

He must be disappointed
And introspect
From disrespect
If the blessing come
But does not succumb to action
Words
If not bare like souls
Shared with world

So I wake in this morning
And I write
Write words about words
About meanings
And emotions
That tell the world
About how I been
About how I being
In definition
A manifestation
Of
Words

Indulge

It is possible
That greatness!
To be it, live it
Inhale and become it,
To allow it in
And exhale it out…
As yours!
And it is possible to roar
Louder than sound
Scream when you've found
Self-love,
Indulge
Your greatness!
Your infinite possibilities…
Claim his greatness…
Inside!

And it's about

It's about the connection between
What is
Understood
And what is not
About
Making sense of what feels
Out of things that
Don't matter
Out of atoms of joy
After boys
Or girls
Toys
It's about exploring
All those things that disconnect
Somehow
In jest
To some of the smaller things
That stand between
Sit in admiration
Celebrate
And make up
Life
It's about

Loss
And
It's about
You

WRIGHT

Life coach
Quit
Had coffee with
Strangers
Tussled with priorities
Outlast the fast
And now I feast
Prayed for fear
To quiet the beast
And then I woke up
Sat up
And dreamed
And
Begin to write again

Aged

When muscle not strength
Begins to hide
And not the journey
But the rides
Begin to change
But experienced smiles
Dial up their power
Like flowers blooming
With love still assuming
All the best
You're not old
Just wiser
Inside

Surface

The carpetbagger
Of encasement
I say that with amazement
It tickles my intellect
To lose all retrospect
Or not believe in karma
At least not beyond
Your own

What death

What joy must be
Painted in melancholy
Wrapped around sunshine
Benign to such stress
And the best
What
Death

Quest

Blindfold
What you won't share
And never bare
Or expose without care
That which has often avoided you
That has become you
In your quest for it
To be, become it
To see and feel it
But
It too is blind
And beautiful
Hurtful
And unsure

CRAVEN

She called it summer snow
And thought I didn't know
That it was the dapper of dawn
Beyond strong
A long one-way relation
She called it her sanity
Her clarity
Even her vanity
In a world insane
Claiming retribution
She stood in confusion
Addicted
Pretending and defending
Virtual realities
True

ABOUT THE AUTHOR

Leo Shelton's Deep Breaths is his fourth published book of poetry, following the 2008 IPPY Award in Poetry for RHYTHMS – Poetry and Muse, as well as Soul-full – Poetry and Deliberate Ramblings. He is a free-lance author and poet, consultant, professor and educator, originally from Nashville, Tennessee, who has lived in the Washington, DC area for over 10 years. He holds several advance degrees and is currently pursuing his doctorate.

Tugson Press
P.O. Box 429
Temple Hills, MD 20757
www.tugsonpress.com